Overcoming Walls to Witnessing

Previously published in 1993 by the Billy Graham Evangelistic Association and adapted from WETN Radio Broadcast by Dr. Timothy Beougher.

This revised edition copyright © 2021 by Timothy K Beougher

First published in Great Britain in 2021

British Library Cataloguing in Publication Data
A record for this book is available from the British Library

ISBN: 978-1-913896-14-0

Designed by Jude May
Cover image © LM-Photo | iStock

Printed in Denmark by Nørhaven

10Publishing, a division of 10ofthose.com
Unit C, Tomlinson Road, Leyland, PR25 2DY, England
Email: info@10ofthose.com
Website: www.10ofthose.com

"Many Christians are not sharing their faith because of various 'walls to witnessing'. I know of no one who can confront these barriers in personal evangelism more winsomely than Dr Tim Beougher. What a privilege to sit at his feet and learn from him in this booklet!"

Dr Robert E. Coleman, author, *The Master Plan of Evangelism*

"Tim Beougher is both scholar and practitioner. As a seminary student where Dr Beougher taught, I enrolled in nearly every course he offered and was never disappointed. His ability to weave sound theology, practical instruction, and inspiring stories has been a help to many aspiring witnesses for Christ. His booklet, *Overcoming Walls to Witnessing*, is one that every Christian should read. It will encourage those believers who feel that witnessing for Christ is something they can never do, as well as equip those who have grown stale in personal evangelism. I have given away numerous copies and those who read it will want to do the same."

Todd Gray, Executive Director-Treasurer for The Kentucky Baptist Convention

"In this slim volume, Tim Beougher confronts six of the most common barriers to personal witnessing with biblical clarity and sanctified common sense. Even after a lifetime of seeking to share my faith, I found *Overcoming*

Walls to Witnessing a powerful motivation to renew my zeal for evangelism. I pray it gains a wide readership."

Al Jackson, Pastor, Lakeview Baptist Church, Alabama

"Tim Beougher is an evangelist to the core and a passionate teacher of evangelism. *Overcoming Walls to Witnessing* is a tried, true, and trustworthy guide to greater effectiveness in sharing Christ with unbelievers. This is a really helpful book, and I am thankful it will serve a new generation, bearing witness to the unchained gospel of Christ."

R. Albert Mohler, Jr, President of The Southern Baptist Theological Seminary

"When I first read the booklet, *Overcoming Walls to Witnessing*, I saw myself in the mirror and I did not like what I saw. I knew beyond any doubt that I was guilty of running into one of the walls of witnessing, the wall of busyness. The words in the booklet were convicting and persuasive. I renewed my commitment to share the gospel more obediently and more faithfully. Get this booklet in the hands of all your church members. Ask them to read it. Ask them to pray about it. And ask them to be obedient to how God speaks to them through it."

Thom S. Rainer, author, former President of LifeWay, and Founder and CEO, Church Answers

TIMOTHY K. BEOUGHER

Overcoming Walls to Witnessing

10 Publishing
a division of 10ofthose.com

Contents

Introduction

Why don't Christians witness more often to the reality of their faith? Or to personalize the question, why don't you witness more regularly— why don't I? This is an important question for each of us to consider as we seek to understand what it means to be a committed follower of Jesus Christ.

Some time ago a survey was taken of those attending evangelism training sessions at a Billy Graham Crusade held in North America.[1] One of the questions on the survey asked, "What is your greatest hindrance in witnessing?" How would you answer that question?

The following are the responses of those attending the training sessions:

---

1. Leighton Ford, *Good News is for Sharing* (David C. Cook Publishing: Elgin, Illinois, 1977), 15.

• More than 50% of those surveyed said their biggest problem was fear of how the other person would react.

• Over 25% said they felt they didn't know enough to share the Gospel adequately.

• Others said they were too busy, not really caring about others, and that their own lives were not consistent enough to share with others.

In the following chapters, we will examine each of these "walls to witnessing" and discover how we can overcome these walls to be more consistent in our witness for Christ. Chapter by chapter, we will look at how to break the barriers that hinder our Christian witness. These barriers include:

1. Breaking the Barrier of Fear, or "I'm afraid to witness."

2. Breaking the Barrier of Giftedness, or "I don't have the gift of evangelism."

3. Breaking the Barrier of Ignorance, or "I don't know how to witness."

4. Breaking the Barrier of Apathy, or "I lack the desire to witness."

5. Breaking the Barrier of Introspection, or "First I need to get my own life in order."

6. Breaking the Barrier of Busyness, or "I can't ever find the time."

Breaking the Barrier of Fear

Fear seems to be the greatest of all barriers to overcome in witnessing. How can we break the barrier of fear in our witnessing?

Struggles with Fear

The first step toward breaking the barrier of fear in our witnessing is to recognize that every Christian struggles with fear in one form or another. We are not alone! All believers who share Christ with others have to work through the issue of fear.

The second step toward breaking the barrier of fear in our witnessing is to identify exactly what our fears are. What is it specifically that we fear?

• Some people fear not knowing enough. We will deal with this issue in Chapter 3 on Breaking the Barrier of Ignorance.

• Some people fear that in their attempt to witness they will do more harm than good. Oftentimes the people who raise this issue are the very ones who have the least to worry about. Why? Because they are the most sensitive when it comes to other people. But we must look at this objection more closely and ask a serious question. How can we possibly place the person into any worse condition? The Bible teaches that people without faith in Christ are lost, and they are doomed to eternity apart from God in hell. Sin brings separation from God. The Bible states, "For the wages of sin is death, but the gift of God is eternal life in Christ Jesus our Lord" (Romans 6:23). This death is known as the "second death," the "lake of fire" or "hell" which is the final destination for all lost humankind (see Revelation 20:15).

• A third fear many Christians struggle with is the fear of rejection. How will the person respond to my witness? Will he or she reject the message? Will he or she reject me? This is perhaps the most common fear.

Sources of Fear

The next step in breaking the barrier of fear is to understand the most common sources of fear. A primary source of fear in our witnessing is Satan. The devil is in the business of erecting walls to prevent us from sharing our faith effectively. Perhaps his greatest workmanship can be seen in the walls of fear he builds around us. Satan knows the tremendous power of the Gospel. He knows that people may respond if they hear and understand the Good News. Therefore, his strategy is to try and hinder Christians from sharing the Gospel with those who need to hear.

Another possible source of fear is a recognition of the enormity of the task of witnessing. It is easy to talk about the weather or gardening or sports. But the more deeply we feel about something and the more personal it is, the more reluctant we may be to talk about it.

And there is nothing more important than a person's eternal destiny! Even when we understand that we are not responsible for a person's response to the Gospel, we still can be overwhelmed when we realize that eternal life is at stake in this person's decision. If we have no hesitation in discussing eternal matters, then perhaps we don't really understand the magnitude of the issue.

A third source of fear, and one we must face openly and honestly, is that most of us have too great a focus on ourselves. We each need to answer this important question, "Will I let fear rule my life, or will I let Jesus Christ rule my life?" Our Lord said, "If anyone would come after Me, he must deny himself and take up his cross and follow Me" (Matthew 16:24). Like Him, we are called to serve others rather than ourselves. We each need to examine our lives and ask, "What can I do daily to serve others as Christ would lead me to do?" When we put Christ first in everything we do, then our focus is on Him rather than on ourselves. If we are willing to follow His direction, the Lord will show us how and where to serve Him.

Responses to Fear

Having identified the problems, the fourth step in breaking the barrier of fear is to understand and apply proper responses to fear. What are these responses?

The first response is to recognize that to a certain degree fear is normal and even desirable. Fear itself is not the problem. Fear can be helpful and even necessary to keep us alert and in a spirit of prayer. Fear can be a good thing when it leads us to have a strong confidence in God, not in ourselves. But when fear keeps us from necessary action, it becomes a problem. When confronted by fear in a witnessing situation, we should see our fear as a blinking red light that the Holy Spirit uses to get our attention so He can remind us, "Trust in Me! Trust in Me! Trust in Me!"

The second response to fear is to recognize that most of our fears are ungrounded. People generally do not respond in a hostile manner. Most non-Christians are far more willing and even eager to discuss spiritual things than Christians think they are! Sometimes their facade (which seems to suggest they are happy and fulfilled) actually shows how hurting and searching they really are.

Of course, it's true that a few people may be hostile. Some may be indifferent. But the fear that people are going to reject us and act negatively is usually not realized. Most people, if approached in a sensitive manner, will react with politeness and interest.

A third response to fear is to remember that fear does not disqualify or excuse us from our responsibility to witness. Even if people do respond in a less than positive manner, that doesn't excuse us. If we plan to wait until all fear is gone before we share God's love with others, then we will never share. Fear will always be with us. But the Good News of the Bible is that fear doesn't need to control us.

Over and over again in the Bible, we are urged, "Do not be afraid" (see John 14:27 and Isaiah 44:8). In commanding us not to fear, Jesus tells us we have a choice in the matter. We can choose not to be afraid, even in the face of fear. We do not need to be afraid when we understand that the Lord is with us each time we witness to someone. Psalm 118:6 says, "The Lord is with me; I will not be afraid. What can man do to me?"

A fourth response to fear is to appropriate God's resources to deal with fear. What are these resources? Through Scripture, we see that God has given us many resources to deal with fear. In 2 Timothy 1:7, Paul reminds Timothy of a fact important to any Christian who takes seriously his or her responsibility to witness. "For God did not give us a spirit of timidity," he wrote, "but a spirit of power, of love and of self-discipline."

God's Resources to Deal with Fear

The first resource God has provided is power. Power overcomes our fear of inadequacy. Boldness is God-given courage that overcomes fear and produces freedom in sharing the Gospel. As believers, we are empowered by the Holy Spirit. Acts 1:8 reads, "But you will receive power when the Holy Spirit comes on you; and you [shall] be My witnesses in Jerusalem, and in all Judea and Samaria, and to the ends of the earth."

We tend to focus on the strategy and forget the power. But the strategy is worthless without the power. This requires a continual infilling of the Holy Spirit.

Do you feel inadequate in evangelism? That's okay! God never intended for us to feel adequate. Scripture tells us His power is perfected in our weakness. 2 Corinthians 4:7 reads, "But we have this treasure in jars of clay to show that this all-surpassing power is from God and not from us." Do you feel inadequate? Great! Then you are a perfect candidate for God's power.

We see this truth displayed many times in the early church. The Apostle Paul tells us in 1 Corinthians 2:3 that he ministered in "weakness and fear, and with much trembling." Paul realized he didn't have it in himself to witness, and he yielded himself to God. It is only when we realize we are not sufficient to do the work of evangelism that God can use us.

Think of the big, brave fisherman Peter. When he tried to rely on his own strength, he denied Christ when questioned by a tiny servant girl (see Mark 14:66–70). But look at his boldness later in life. When dragged before the religious authorities and ordered not to speak any more about Jesus, Peter and the other apostles replied, "We must obey God rather than men!" (Acts 5:29). Peter learned to rely on God's power instead of his own.

In Acts 4:18–20, we see Peter and John arrested and commanded not to speak or teach at all in the name of Jesus. After they had been threatened, they and the other disciples prayed for boldness. Notice they did not pray for safety—they prayed for boldness to enable them to continue sharing in the face of opposition. Why did they pray for boldness? Because they needed it! You don't pray for something you already have. And they received boldness because they prayed for it.

Later on, in Acts 5:28–29, we see them again dragged before the authorities. The high priest said, "We gave you strict orders not to teach in this name. ... Yet you have filled Jerusalem with your teaching." Take note that this is what their enemies said about them.

What did they do? They continued to share Christ even under the shadow of persecution, because they had prayed for and received boldness. Did they struggle with fear? No doubt! But they were more concerned that lost people hear the message of the Gospel than with their own safety. They continued to share Christ boldly.

How is boldness produced? Acts 4 suggests three ways:

1. Verse 13 suggests that boldness is produced through personal contact with Jesus. As we spend time with Him daily, He supplies us with His strength and power.

2. Verses 29–31 show us that boldness is also given in response to our prayers.

3. Verse 31 teaches us that boldness is a by-product of being filled with the Holy Spirit. God gives us His power to break the barrier of fear.

The second resource God has provided is love, which is the best antidote to fear. Love overcomes our fear of rejection and leads us to forget our own fears and focus on the needs of others. 1 John 4:18 states that "perfect love drives out fear."

We see this demonstrated in Paul's ministry in Thessalonica, recorded in 1 Thessalonians 2:1–8. This passage tells us the reasons for Paul's boldness were twofold:

1. He was convinced his message was from God.

2. He was concerned about people—he loved the people to whom he was ministering. His motive was not to serve himself but to serve others in a spirit of love.

The third resource God has provided is discipline. Discipline overcomes our fear of failure. We must discipline ourselves to learn how to share the Gospel, spend time in prayer, spend time with non-Christians, and take advantage of opportunities to reach out with the love of Christ. We then reach out to others with the full confidence that our Lord is working both in us and through us to bring people to Himself.

How are we to apply these things? How can power, love, and discipline become a reality in our lives instead of fear? We must learn to see things as God sees them. We must daily resist being conformed to this world, but instead be transformed by the renewing of our minds, as Romans 12:2 instructs us. We must learn to say as Paul does in 2 Corinthians 5:11, "Since, then, we know what it is to fear the Lord, we try to persuade men."

An attitude of fear is not consistent with the resources God has promised His children. The Christian's response to fear must be faith. If you feel inadequate in trying to reach out to others, God wants to teach you His adequacy. In 2 Corinthians 2:14–16, we read, "But thanks be to God, who always leads us in triumphal procession in Christ and through us spreads everywhere the fragrance of the knowledge of Him. For we are to God the aroma of Christ among those who are being saved and those who are perishing. To the one we are the smell of death; to the other, the fragrance of life. And who is equal to such a task?"

Paul answers the question he has just asked a few verses later in 2 Corinthians 3:5– 6, "Not that we are competent in ourselves to claim anything for ourselves, but our competence comes from God. He has made us competent as ministers of a new covenant—not of the letter but of the Spirit; for the letter kills, but the Spirit gives life."

As I mentioned earlier, when you are afraid, view that as a blinking red light with the Holy Spirit saying, "Trust in Me! Trust in Me! Trust in Me!" Then step out in faith.

Fear knocked at the door. Faith answered. There was no one there.[2]

---

2. The World Treasury of Religious Quotations (Hawthorne Books, Inc.: New York, New York, November, 1966), 331.

Breaking the Barrier of Giftedness

A hindrance to evangelism not pinpointed in the survey done by the Billy Graham Association in 1976 but that I find frequently mentioned today relates to the "gift of evangelism." The logic goes something like this: "Evangelism is a spiritual gift; I don't have that spiritual gift; therefore, God does not expect me to do evangelism."

Is There a "Gift of Evangelism?"

Evangelism (or at least the word "evangelism") is not listed as a spiritual gift in the three major lists of spiritual gifts in the New Testament (e.g. Romans 12:6–8; 1 Corinthians 12:7–10, 27–31; and Ephesians 4:11). Kenneth Gangel argues since the term "evangelist" is used in Ephesians 4:11, it most likely signifies an office and not a gift.[3] Juan M. Isais argues that evangelism should not be seen as a spiritual gift: "…in the Bible…there is no such thing as the gift of evangelism…"[4]

Others assume that evangelism is a spiritual gift.[5] Larry Gilbert not only declares there is a gift of evangelism, but he also seeks to define the gift in terms of its function:

> There was a time when I might have had to
> spend a lot of time arguing the point that there
> is a **gift** of evangelism. Thankfully, today,
> most people believe that God has given a gift to
> certain people that allows them to be more

---

3. See Kenneth Gangel, *Unwrap Your Spiritual Gifts* (Wheaton, IL: Victor Books, 1983).

4. Juan M. Isais, "The Gift Which Does Not Exist in the Bible," in *The Other Evangelism* (Winona Lake, IN: Brethren Evangelistic Ministries, 1989), 22-23.

5. Thomas R. Schreiner, *Spiritual Gifts: What They Are & Why They Matter* (Nashville, TN: B&H Publishing Group, 2018), 25-26. Schreiner does not note the distinction between the words "evangelism" and "evangelist"; he simply states, "Some have the gift of evangelism (Eph. 4:11)." For others who affirm a spiritual gift of evangelism, see John Walvoord, *The Holy Spirit at Work Today* (Chicago, IL: Moody Press, 1943), 40; and Leslie B. Flynn, *19 Gifts of the Spirit* (Wheaton, IL: Victor Books, 1976), 56-65.

aggressive, confrontational, and outgoing in their witnessing. The gifted evangelist can lead people to Christ far easier than the average Christian. Nearly 10 percent of all church members have this special gift.[6]

Quite frankly, I think this issue remains an open question. While I cannot argue definitively *against* evangelism being a spiritual gift, I certainly cannot argue definitively that evangelism *is* a spiritual gift.

Even If Evangelism Is a "Gift," It Is Also Clearly a Command for All Believers

I once heard a speaker tell a large Christian audience, "If you don't have the gift of evangelism, stop feeling guilty about not witnessing. You will serve God in other ways besides evangelism. But that doesn't let you off the hook. You need to pray for those who do have the gift of evangelism. But stop feeling guilty if witnessing isn't your thing."

I had the opportunity to talk with this speaker afterward, and I asked him if I could come and

---

6. Larry Gilbert, *Team Evangelism: Outreach for the 90% Who Don't Have the Gift of Evangelism* (Lynchburg, VA: Church Growth Institute, 1991), 13.

speak at his church for two consecutive Sundays. The first Sunday I wanted to stand in front of his congregation and ask, "How many of you have ever felt guilty about giving? I am here today to relieve you of that guilt. If you don't have the gift of giving, God doesn't expect you to give. But you need to pray for those who do have the gift, and please pray hard, because this church has a large budget."

The second Sunday I would ask, "How many of you have felt guilty about not serving?", and when I see the large number of hands raised, I would continue: "I am here today to relieve you of that guilt. If you don't have the gift of serving, God doesn't expect you to serve. But you need to pray for those who do have the gift, and please pray hard, because each of those people will be wearing about twenty-seven hats in this church."

This man begrudgingly conceded I might have a point. I assured him I did have a point! We know there are gifts of giving and serving, and yet God calls all believers to participate in those actions. Even if evangelism is a spiritual gift, it is clearly a command for all believers.

Do Christians See Themselves As "On-Mission" for Christ?

What do you call someone who works at a hospital assisting doctors? A nurse, correct? Suppose that nurse is a believer and flies to the Philippines to serve. What do we call them then? A medical missionary, correct? Why do we not see them as a medical missionary here? Why do they perhaps not see themselves as a medical missionary here?

Years ago, I was visiting a church and overheard a conversation that crystalized my thinking on this issue. One woman asked another woman, "What do you do?" The second woman replied: "What do I do? I am a disciple of the Lord Jesus Christ, on mission for Him, cleverly disguised as an emergency room nurse!" I thought, that is the perspective we all need to have.

This identity is what we must cultivate in our own lives. What do you do? I'm a disciple of the Lord Jesus Christ, on mission for Him, cleverly disguised as a teacher, stay-at-home mom, construction worker, college student, engineer, secretary, factory worker, etc. Is that how you view yourself?

We can overcome the barrier of giftedness by realizing that regardless of what our spiritual gifts are (or are not), all believers are called to be witnesses for Christ. Let me suggest four reasons why all Christians should be involved in evangelism, regardless of their gifting.

1. The commands to witness are given to all followers of Christ.

Acts 1:8, for example, reads, "But you will receive power when the Holy Spirit has come upon you, and you will be my witnesses in Jerusalem and in all Judea and Samaria, and to the end of the earth." This verse gives a command from the risen Lord to all His followers. As John Stott argues, "We can no more restrict the command to witness than we can restrict the promise of the Spirit."[7]

In writing to the Corinthian believers, Paul maintained:

All this is from God, who reconciled us to himself through Christ and gave us the ministry of reconciliation: that God was reconciling the world to himself in Christ, not counting people's sins against them. And he has committed to us

---

7. John R.W. Stott, *Our Guilty Silence* (Downers Grove, IL: Inter-Varsity Press, 1967), 58.

> *the message of reconciliation. We are therefore*
> *Christ's ambassadors, as though God were*
> *making his appeal through us. We implore you*
> *on Christ's behalf: Be reconciled to God.*

Not only do apostles have the ministry of reconciliation and the role of Christ's ambassadors, but all believers also have this responsibility. Other verses that reflect on this ministry of witnessing for all believers include Matthew 5:14–16, 1 Peter 3:15, Philippians 2:14–16, Colossians 4:5–6 and 1 Peter 2:9.[8]

2. "Ordinary believers" in the early church shared the Gospel.

As we follow the storyline of the early church, it is obvious that the apostles sought to evangelize and disciple others. But we see ordinary believers sharing the Gospel as well. Following the stoning of Stephen, we read in Acts 8:1, "And there arose on that day a great persecution against the church in Jerusalem, and they were all scattered throughout

---

8. While the context of 1 Peter 3:15 is what can be called "passive evangelism" (i.e. responding to a question that an unbeliever asks), this command is clearly given to all believers "to be ready" to answer when asked.

the regions of Judea and Samaria, except the apostles." And what did those ordinary believers do? Acts 8:4 tells us: "Now those who were scattered went about preaching *[euangelizomenoi]* the word." They went about sharing the Gospel with others!

Noted historian Kenneth Scott Latourette makes this observation about the spread of the Gospel: "The chief agents in the expansion of Christianity appear not to have been those who made it a profession or a major part of their occupation, but men and women who earned their livelihood in some purely secular manner and spoke of their faith to those whom they met in this natural fashion."[9]

3. All believers must steward the Gospel.

Luke 12:48 reminds us that "everyone to whom much is given, of him much will be required." We have been given the greatest gift of the gospel, and have no greater stewardship than to share that message of Good News with others. Paul expresses it well in 2 Corinthians 5:14: "for the love of Christ controls us."

---

9. Kenneth Scott Latourette, *A History of the Expansion of Christianity* (New York, NY: Harper & Brothers, 1937), 1:116.

4. The "work of ministry" in Ephesians 4 is for everyone.

Paul makes note of different offices in the church (apostles, prophets, evangelists, shepherds, and teachers) and declares part of the reason God "gifts" the church with such leaders is so they will "…equip the saints for the work of ministry, for building up the body of Christ" (Ephesians 4:12). Among all the ministries reflected in that phrase "the work of ministry," evangelism surely must be included.

Those who have a particular gift of evangelism aren't given the gift just for their own witness but to help equip each and every believer to share the Gospel regardless of their particular gifting. Some people run from the idea of evangelism because they assume it means they must be obnoxious and pushy. There are many methods of witnessing, many approaches to sharing the Gospel. The only fixed "method" is the "message"—telling others about the Gospel of Jesus Christ. Let's share Christ's love with great passion and with great joy!

Breaking the Barrier of Ignorance

When people say they don't know how to witness, it usually means one of two things. It may mean they are unclear about the message of the Gospel, or they are uncertain about an appropriate method to share the message.

Clarifying the Message

Why are some Christians unclear about the message of the Gospel? It seems obvious that we must know the message of the Gospel in order to share it. We must have personally experienced the love of God through Christ because it is impossible to proclaim a faith we do not possess. An experiential knowledge of God through Christ is essential to effective witnessing. When people have experienced the redeeming love of God for themselves, they have something to share! The very word witness, as defined by Webster's Dictionary, is someone "who has personal knowledge of something" and who gives a "public affirmation by word or example."[10]

Some people know for certain that they have trusted Christ as their Lord and Savior; yet, they are not sure how to explain the Gospel message. To overcome the barrier of ignorance, we must know and be thoroughly convinced of the importance of the message we are sharing with others. As Paul wrote to Timothy, we must "know whom [we] have believed ..." (2 Timothy 1:12).

There are many "summaries" of the Gospel that have proven helpful to Christians as they seek to communicate the Good News of Jesus Christ. Such summaries as "The Roman Road," "The Four Spiritual Laws," and the "Bridge Illustration" utilize key verses to help persons identify the essentials of the Gospel message.

Some have attempted to help people understand the Gospel by breaking it down into four steps:

10. Webster's New Collegiate Dictionary (G. & C, Merriam Company: Springfield, Massachusetts, 1981), 1337.

God's design, our sin, Christ's provision, and our response. God's design was for people to live in fellowship with Him and with one another. But sin marred that relationship, and fellowship with God was broken. Christ Himself (fully God and fully man) came to earth and was crucified, buried, and rose again to provide the only way to pay the penalty for our sin. Christ offers eternal life to all who will respond to Him in repentance and faith. For those who desire further reading to help clarify the Gospel message, see the list of books in the resource section on page 91.

Choosing the Method

What about those people who feel they know the message of the Gospel, but are struggling with an appropriate method to share Christ with others? There are a variety of methods. No one particular method is the right one when it comes to evangelism. But there is a wrong method—to sit back and do nothing.

D. L. Moody, a revival preacher, was confronted one day by a person who disapproved of his method of witnessing. Moody replied that he wasn't overly fond of it himself and asked, "What methods do you use?" "Oh, I don't have a method," the critic replied. "Well," Moody retorted, "I think I like the way I do it better than the way you don't!"[11]

Too many people get sidetracked in debates over methodology. It is worthwhile to note that Jesus used different methods when healing blind men. On one occasion He merely spoke a word (Mark 10:52), and on another, He placed mud on the blind man's eyes (John 9:6). Can you imagine what might have transpired had these men happened to meet together to discuss their experiences?

"Isn't it wonderful how Jesus heals by simply speaking?" one would say. "No, He uses mud. Don't you know that is the best method?" the other would reply. If they had been like some of our modern churches, they might have split off and formed two new denominations: the "Muddites" and the "Anti-Muddites"![12]

What Are the Methods?

For those who are confused about different methods or are not sure how to begin witnessing, an evangelistic tool such as a Gospel booklet or

---

11. Leighton Ford, *The Christian Persuader* (Harper & Row, Publishers: New York, New York, 1966), 68.
12. Ford, 125.

tract is a good way to start. An evangelistic tool has several advantages in witnessing. It can give you confidence when you may be nervous, as it has the appropriate Gospel verses printed out in case you forget them. It presents the Gospel clearly without getting sidetracked on other issues. Most give visual help as well as verbal, and they offer suggestions for Christian growth. Another significant benefit to using evangelistic tools in witnessing is that the non-Christian will then have something to keep, so he or she can look it over later. There are many fine booklets on the market to help Christians in their witnessing. You can find a wide selection at 10ofThose.com, at your local church, or wherever Christian books are sold.[13]

Another popular method for sharing the Gospel is to utilize your personal testimony. A personal testimony is simply telling the story of how you became a Christian and what Christ has done in your life since then. This can be a significant method because it is easy to share the story of your own spiritual pilgrimage. Also, it helps others to be more willing to share their lives with you.

---

13. The booklet I recommend is "Experiencing God's Grace", a booklet I helped develop. It is available from 10ofthose.com

We see a beautiful example of the use of personal testimony from the life of the Apostle Paul. It can be broken down in the following way:

• First, Paul's life before he becomes a Christian (Acts 22:3–5).

• Second, Paul becomes a Christian (Acts 22:7–16).

• Third, Paul's life after becoming a Christian (Acts 22:21).

This provides an excellent pattern for us to follow as we seek to communicate what Christ has done in our own lives. In addition to this general outline, the following are a few other helpful hints in sharing your personal testimony:

• Present your testimony in a way where others can identify.

• Share your weaknesses and needs openly and honestly with them.

• Use Scripture in your testimony where appropriate.

• Stress the nature of the personal relationship you have with Christ right now.

• Try to avoid using religious language which may not be familiar to a non-Christian.

• Do not give the impression that the Christian life is a "bed of roses" and that you are now perfect. Paint an accurate picture.

• Above all, make sure the emphasis in your testimony is Christ and the Gospel, not yourself. No one is saved simply by hearing stories from our past; they are saved by hearing and responding to the Gospel message.

God Uses Ordinary People

Even with these bits of help, how do we overcome the barrier of ignorance when it comes to sharing our faith? Ultimately, we must all begin where we are and then seek to grow. Anyone who knows Jesus can bear witness to Him. Many of the people in Bible times who testified of Jesus had no training, formal or otherwise, in the Scriptures or in witnessing.

One such person was the woman of Samaria who left her water pots and told her fellow villagers about Jesus. She had never experienced a call to ministry, had not attended a single seminary class, and had never read a book on witnessing. What she did have was a personal encounter with the Savior of the world, and from her personal meeting, she eagerly went to share with others (see John 4:4–42).

The Bible tells us in John 9 of another time when God used an ordinary person to witness. One of the blind men whom Jesus healed was questioned by the Pharisees about the event. This man replied, "Whether He [Jesus] is a sinner or not, I don't know. One thing I do know. I was blind but now I see!" (John 9:25). Here was another person with no formal training or experience in evangelism. Yet Scripture shows him witnessing to the religious elite of his day! He could not have discussed the finer points of theology with them, but he was able to bear witness to the person and work of Jesus Christ.

Training Opportunities

Finally, if you really desire to learn more about witnessing, there is an abundance of training opportunities available. What are some opportunities to learn? Physical or online Christian bookstores are stocked with many excellent books on the subject of witnessing. For a list of some suggested books on witnessing, see the resource section on page 91. Also, you may want to ask your pastor and Christian friends for other titles they would recommend. Beyond personal reading, many churches offer training programs for those interested in learning how to share their faith. By making a few brief inquiries at your own church and churches in the area, you should be able to locate various opportunities to learn. Begin praying that God would open doors for you to share Christ with others. This is a prayer He delights to answer.

How, then, are you to break the barrier of ignorance? You should certainly seek further knowledge and training, but the bottom line is to begin where you are at this moment. If you wait until you have mastered every approach, anticipated every question, read every book, etc., you will never witness. You may feel there is so much more you could know about sharing your faith. By all means, take advantage of opportunities to learn more. But don't let that stop you from beginning where you are and reaching out to others right now.

A True Story

A modern-day news story tells how one "ordinary" man responded in a crisis to save a drowning woman.[14] This true story illustrates the need for Christians to act now to rescue the lost. The event took place on January 13, 1982, when Air Florida's Flight 90 crashed on takeoff and fell into the icy waters of the Potomac River. Martin Skutnik, age twenty-eight, saw the plane go down. He stood with other spectators on the riverbank watching a woman who had survived the crash and was struggling to swim in the cold water.

Skutnik plunged into the river and rescued her. He had never taken a life-saving course, but he saved the woman's life. He probably didn't use proper form or technique when he swam to the woman's side, at least as professional swim instructors would teach it. He may not have followed the Red Cross's Lifesaving Manual in the method he used to grab the woman and bring her back to the safety of the shore. At that time, Skutnik was a general office worker. He had a wife and two children and lived in a rented townhouse. He had no training for the task he undertook that day. But he couldn't stand by idly and let another human being die without trying to help.

---

14. James J. Kilpatrick, "Rescuer's Name Could Be Legion, For He is Many," *The Kansas City Times* (Kansas City, Kansas: January 22, 1982), A-9.

He became a national hero on that fateful day by risking his life to rescue that drowning woman.

You may feel less than adequate for the task of witnessing about Christ's love to those around you. You may feel inadequate because of your lack of formal training. Yet, like Martin Skutnik, the urgency of the moment demands that you do what you can with what you have right now. Yes, seek to learn all you can about witnessing, seek to improve your skills in communicating the Gospel, but don't wait until you think you've got it all together to begin sharing. The Gospel is the Good News! Will you seek to share it with someone today?

Breaking the Barrier of Apathy

Herein is a mystery. The Bible shows that it often takes God longer to get a Christian ready to witness than it does to get a lost person ready to be saved. The Bible highlights three factors in the conversion of any person: The Gospel of Christ, the Holy Spirit, and the agency of humans. The first two of these are always found to be active in the conversion process. The Gospel is the power of God unto salvation. The Holy Spirit is at work, convicting people of sin, righteousness and judgment. What is the missing ingredient? It is the factor of human agency. What is lacking is a willing witness.

Emotions and the Will

Before we discuss the importance of having a burden for evangelism, we need to recognize one important truth. The Christian life was never intended to be lived solely in the realm of emotion. Yes, emotions are God-given and can be a powerful means by which He stirs us to action. But Scripture emphasizes that our decisions must come from the will. We are to choose God's way whether or not we feel particularly good about following it at that time.

If we try to base our actions on emotions, ultimately, we will be frustrated. The mountaintop and valley experiences of the Christian life are not the norm; most of the Christian life is lived on the plain. We need to learn to make choices based on what we know is right, not because we feel good on the inside about doing them.

Burdened for Evangelism

Having recognized this important truth, we must also acknowledge that having a burden for the lost can be a powerful motivation in our witness. Douglas Stewart has said the single greatest reason we fail to witness is that we do not possess the compassion of Christ.[15] Arthur C. Archibald believed the most powerful ingredient in our

---

15. Douglas Stewart, "Evangelism," *The Expository Times*, 67 (July 1956), 312.

evangelism was "a deep sense of concern."[16] John Henry Jowett emphasizes the importance of compassion by saying, "The Gospel of a broken heart demands the ministry of bleeding hearts. ... As soon as we cease to bleed, we cease to bless. ...Tearless hearts can never be the heralds of the Passion."[17]

What exactly do we mean when we use the term compassion? The word comes from the Latin "passion," meaning to suffer or to feel, and the prefix "con," meaning with.[18] Thus, when we have compassion, we suffer or feel with someone.

Scripture gives us many examples of those who demonstrated a heart of compassion for others. For example, Moses said to the Lord, "Oh, what a great sin these people have committed! They have made themselves gods of gold. But now, please forgive their sin—but if not, then blot me out of the book you have written" (Exodus 32:31–32).

---

16. Arthur C. Archibald, *New Testament Evangelism* (Judson Press: Philadelphia, Pennsylvania, 1946), 113.

17. John Henry Jowett, *The Passion for Souls* (Fleming H. Revell Company: New York, 1905), 30 & 34.

18. *Webster's New Collegiate Dictionary* (G. & C. Merriam Company: Springfield, Massachusetts, 1981), 831.

The Apostle Paul displayed a similar heart of compassion. We see his deep concern for others when he said, "I have great sorrow and unceasing anguish in my heart. For I could wish that I myself were cursed and cut off from Christ for the sake of my brothers, those of my own race, the people of Israel" (Romans 9:2–3).

The supreme example of compassion for others is, of course, our Lord Jesus Christ. Matthew 9:36 records that when He saw the multitudes, "He had compassion on them." Luke 19:41 presents Jesus approaching the city of Jerusalem and weeping over it. The shortest verse in the English Bible, John 11:35, simply says, "Jesus wept." Perhaps we have heard it emphasized so much as the shortest verse in the Bible that we have missed the very point of the verse—Jesus had a deep concern and compassion for people. Why is it that so many of us who claim to follow the Compassionate One are so lacking in compassion? God may need to break our hardness of heart and lack of concern.

Others who have been used by God throughout history have had this sense of burden for lost people. John Vassar, the great evangelist who ministered in Boston, once knocked on the door of a woman's home and asked if she knew Christ as her Savior.[19]

She said, "It's none of your business," and slammed the door in his face. He stood on the doorstep for a period of time and wept and wept over this woman's condition.

She looked out of her window and saw him standing there, weeping because of her. The next Sunday morning she was in church. The pastor saw her and said he was surprised to see her. She said it was those tears. She couldn't get away from those tears.

Where are our tears? When did we last weep for lost humanity? A few years after the death of the famous preacher, Robert Murray M'Cheyne, a young minister visited his church to discover, as he explained, the secret of the man's amazing influence. The beadle (sexton), who had served under Mr. M'Cheyne, took the youthful inquirer into the vestry and asked him to sit in the chair used by the great preacher.

"Now put your elbows on the table," he said. "Now put your face in your hands." The visitor

19. Billy Graham, "Stains on the Altar," *One Race, One Gospel, One Task* (World Wide Publications: Minneapolis, Minnesota, 1967), 155.

obeyed. "Now let the tears flow! That was the way Mr. M'Cheyne used to do!"

The man then led the minister to the pulpit and gave him a fresh series of instructions. "Put your elbows down on the pulpit!" He put his elbows down. "Now put your face in your hands!" He did as he was told. "Now let the tears flow! That was the way Mr. M'Cheyne used to do!"[20]

Compassion for the Lost

How can we develop this kind of burden for people who don't know Christ? How can we cultivate this kind of compassion in our lives? The fact that you are reading this booklet on evangelism indicates you have some desire to reach out. What can you do to deepen that desire?

The first step in developing a heart of compassion is to honestly face the truth that people outside of Christ are destined for hell, separated from God's love for eternity. People who live and die without knowing Christ are lost. They are lost now, and they will be lost forever. Yes, this is a harsh reality, but it is

---

20. F.W. Boreham, *A Late Lark Singing* (Epworth Press: London, England, 1945), 66, cited in Robert E. Coleman, "Focusing the Message," *Choose Ye This Day* (World Wide: Minneapolis, Minnesota, 1989), 73.

true nevertheless. The existence of hell was taught over and over by Jesus Christ Himself. In Matthew 10:28, Jesus warned, "Do not be afraid of those who kill the body but cannot kill the soul. Rather, be afraid of the One who can destroy both soul and body in hell." In Matthew 25:46, He said, "Then they will go away to eternal punishment [hell], but the righteous to eternal life [heaven]."

Yet, in spite of Jesus' clear teaching on the subject, hell has been abandoned as a doctrine by a large segment of the church. Evangelist, Leighton Ford, has written an article that asks the following question: "Do You Mean to Tell Me that in This Modern, Humanistic, Pluralistic, Tolerant Society You Still Believe in Hell?"[21] Yes, those who follow Jesus Christ as Lord still believe in hell, not because they want to, but because Jesus taught that there is such a place.

But even those who haven't abandoned it as a theological truth often fail to consider its reality. Do we daily consider the horrors of hell? Do we remember that people who die apart from faith in

---

21. Leighton Ford, "Do You Mean to Tell Me that in This Modern, Humanistic, Pluralistic, Tolerant Society You Still Believe in Hell?" *Worldwide Challenge* (Campus Crusade for Christ: San Bernardino, California, September/October, 1983), 20-23.

Christ are headed there? Do we really understand what it means to love our neighbor as we love our own self? If we truly believe in the reality of heaven and hell, we cannot say we truly love someone if we refuse to share the Gospel with them. This point is emphasized in the following comments found in a booklet titled, "Tract Written by an Atheist:"[22]

Did I firmly believe, as millions say they do, that the knowledge and practice of religion in this life influences destiny in another, religion would mean to me everything? I would cast away earthly enjoyments, earthly cares, and earthly thoughts as worthless. Religion would be my first waking thought and my last image before sleep sank me into unconsciousness. I would look at one soul gained for heaven worth a life of suffering. Earthly consequences should never keep my hand from being active in the cause of the Gospel nor seal my lips. I would strive to look upon eternity alone and on the immortal souls around me soon to be everlastingly happy or everlastingly miserable. I would go out into the world and preach, and my text would be

22. Norman P. Grubb, *C. T. Studd* (Fort Washington, Pennsylvania: Christian Literature Crusade, 1933, 1982), 35-36.

*Matthew 16:26, KJV, "What shall it profit a man
if he gain the whole world and lose his own soul?"*

Thousands of people die each day and enter a Christ-less eternity. The question is, "Do we care?" As Christians, we have the message that can save people from this fate—the message that can set them free. We must remember the Gospel is the Good News! People are hungry and waiting. Billy Graham stated that he is finding a receptivity to the Gospel today on a scale never seen before in his many years of ministry. As Jesus said in John 4:35, "I tell you, open your eyes and look at the fields! They are ripe for harvest."

A second step toward cultivating a heart of compassion is to recognize that time is short. James 4:14 reminds us that our life is like "a mist that appears for a little while and then vanishes." Hebrews 9:27 teaches that a person is "destined to die once, and after that to face judgment." George Bernard Shaw once noted that the ultimate statistic is this: "One out of one dies."[23] Have we come to grips with this reality?

---

23. *Gathered Gold: A Treasury of Quotations for Christians*, compiled by John Blanchard (Evangelical Press: Welwyn, England, 1984), 60.

A third means of cultivating a heart of compassion is to spend consistent time in Scripture. D. L. Moody once preached a sermon on compassion.[24] A newspaper reporter asked him, "How did you prepare that sermon?" Moody said that while on his knees he read several passages of Scripture about the compassion of Jesus. As he read, he became overwhelmed with a burden for the lost. He said, "I lay on the floor of my bedroom and prayed, and read, and wept. As I did, I wrote down the thoughts that came to my mind and heart."

A fourth means of developing compassion is to spend time with lost people. Too many Christians have no close non-Christian friends to whom they are reaching out with the love of Christ. As we get involved in the lives of others, we begin to see the heartaches of life firsthand. Then we are moved to reach out to them in love. We may sing on Sunday morning, "Rescue the perishing, care for the dying, snatch them in pity from sin and the grave,"[25] but our actions during

---

24. George Sweeting, "The Evangelist's Passion for the Lost," *The Calling of an Evangelist* (World Wide Pictures: Minneapolis, Minnesota, 1987), 37.

25. Fanny J. Crosby, "Rescue the Perishing," *Hymns for the Family of God*, (Paragon Associates, Inc.: Nashville, Tennessee, 1976), 661.

the week might be proclaiming, "I really couldn't care less."

A fifth means of developing compassion is to spend time in intercessory prayer. Canadian pastor, Oswald J. Smith, has asked, "Can children be born without pain? Can there be birth without travail? Yet how many expect in the spiritual realm that which is not possible in the natural!"[26] We may need to pray, "God, break my heart with the things that break your heart." If we lack a burden for the lost, we should get on our knees and ask God to give it to us.

Allow God to burden you. Remember, God-given burdens are not too heavy to bear, because Jesus Himself enables us to carry them. When we ask God to burden us for the lost, we don't need to fear that we will become overwhelmed and weary with the task of evangelism. The Lord tells us: "Come to me, all you who are weary and burdened, and I will give you rest. Take my yoke upon you and learn from me, for I am gentle and humble in heart, and you will find rest for your souls. For my yoke is easy and my burden is light" (Matthew 11:28–30). Later, in Matthew 12:34,

---

26. Oswald J. Smith, *The Passion For Souls* (Marshall, Morgan, and Scott, LTD.: London, 1950), 26.

Jesus says the mouth speaks of that which fills the heart. Will you allow God to fill your heart with a burden for lost people?

Breaking the Barrier of Introspection

What is the Barrier of Introspection? It can be stated in several ways. Whether it is phrased as "First, I need to get my own life in order," or "I've got enough problems of my own which I need to work on first," or "When I get myself straightened out, then I'll start witnessing," this barrier always points to some future point when everything will suddenly come together in our lives. At that point, we say, we'll reach out to others with the Gospel.

No Perfect Witnesses

The problem with such reasoning is that we will never be perfect in this life! If we must wait until we become "good enough" to begin sharing our faith with others, we will never begin. Spiritual perfection awaits us in another world—heaven. Since there are no perfect Christians here on this earth, there can be no perfect witnesses. If perfection were a necessary qualification, then nobody would make it. The simple fact is that God uses everyone by grace.

Now it is certainly true that our life and lips— our walk and our talk—should agree. Our lives should reflect the message that we proclaim. But while recognizing that we are not perfect in our personal lives, we must nonetheless step out in faith and begin to share the Gospel with others. We cannot delay our witnessing until some "magical" point when we finally think we "have it all together." We never will attain perfection in this life!

Part of the wonder of the Gospel message is that God saves sinners—sinners like you and me. Like the converted slave trader John Newton, we can all identify with the words of the hymn, "Amazing grace, how sweet the sound, that saved a wretch like me."[27] Being a Christian doesn't mean we never stumble, but it does mean we

27. John Newton, "Amazing Grace," *Hymns for the Family of God*, (Paragon Associates, Inc.: Nashville, Tennessee, 1976), 107.

can honestly admit it when we do fail and seek forgiveness from God and others whom we have wronged. This in itself can be a powerful basis for witnessing.

The early Christians certainly did not wait until they had become spiritually perfect before they shared Christ's love with others. The Samaritan woman began telling people immediately about the love of Christ. Jesus did not select highly qualified individuals who had demonstrated deep spiritual insight to be His disciples; He chose rough, uneducated fishermen to tell His story of love.

Someone has highlighted just how "ordinary" the first disciples were by composing a hypothetical memorandum which reads as follows:

TO: Jesus, Son of Joseph, Woodcrafters Shop, Nazareth
FROM: Jordan Management Consultants, Jerusalem
SUBJECT: Staff Aptitude Evaluation

Thank you for submitting the resumes of the twelve men you have picked for management positions in your new organization. All of them have now taken our tests, and we have not only reviewed the results, but also have arranged personal interviews for each of them with our psychologist and vocational aptitude consultant.

It is the staff opinion that most of your nominees are lacking in background, education, and vocational aptitude for the type of enterprise you are undertaking. They do not have the team concept. We would recommend that you continue your search for persons of experience in managerial ability and proven capability.

Simon Peter is emotionally unstable and given to fits of temper. Andrew has absolutely no qualities of leadership. The two brothers, James and John, the sons of Zebedee, place personal interest above company loyalty. Thomas demonstrates a questioning attitude that would tend to undermine morale. We feel that it is our duty to tell you that Matthew has been blacklisted by the Greater Jerusalem Better Business Bureau. James, the son of Alphaeus, and Thaddeus definitely have radical leanings, and they both registered a high score on the manic-depressive scale.

One of the candidates, however, shows great potential. He is a man of ability and resourcefulness, meets people well, has a keen business mind and has contacts in high places. He is highly motivated, ambitious and innovative. We recommend Judas Iscariot as your controller and right-hand man. All the other profiles are self-explanatory. We wish you every success in your new venture.

Sincerely,
Jordan Management Consultants

Were these early disciples perfect? Far from it! But they recognized their inadequacy for the task and learned to rely on God's wisdom and strength. The recognition of our inadequacy can, in fact, contribute to effective witnessing if we remember that it is the Holy Spirit who must work in and through us.

What About Hypocrisy?

Even though we understand that there are no perfect Christians, many in the Christian community have been embarrassed by the scandals that have been front-page news in recent years. Perhaps we are a little more reluctant to share our faith with others because we don't want to open ourselves up to the charge of being a hypocrite. What do we do when someone raises this as an issue?

First, it is important to remember that while consistent living is very important, our lives are not the Gospel. We invite people to trust Christ not because we are perfect Christians but because of who Jesus Christ is and what He has done. If the person you are witnessing to is hung up on the question of hypocrites, admit it!

There are hypocrites in the church just as there are in every other arena of life. Some police officers are crooked. But what happens when someone breaks into your home late at night? Do you reason, "Some police officers are crooked. I'm not about to call the police. How do I know I won't get one who is a hypocrite?" A few physicians are incompetent. But when you face a life-threatening emergency, do you reason, "I'm not about to go to the Emergency Room. What if I get a doctor who is a quack? I'm not about to take that chance; I'm not going to the hospital". Obviously, people don't reason this way in any other area of their lives except when it pertains to the church.

Focus on Christ

It is helpful to focus on the person of Christ. Share with the person that Jesus wasn't a hypocrite. Say, "He hated hypocrisy as much as you apparently do." He reserved some of His harshest words for the religious hypocrites of His day. In Matthew 23, Jesus addressed religious hypocrites using terms such as "blind guides," "blind fools," "snakes," and "brood of vipers." He chastised them for their greed, self-indulgence, and wickedness. No one could say that Jesus ever gave His approval to hypocrisy.

Ultimately, the real issue is not hypocrites in the church but that person's response to Jesus Christ. Romans 14:12 teaches that every person will stand before God to give an account of his or her life. At that time, whether or not others were hypocrites will not matter in the least. Each of us will have to answer to God for our own lives.

We Are Weak/He Is Strong

A second means to overcoming the barrier of introspection is to understand that even a person who is struggling in one or more areas of life can be a powerful witness to the reality of Jesus Christ.

His power can be perfected in our weakness (see 2 Corinthians 12:9). When we are weak, He shows Himself to be strong. Satan tries to whisper to us that we need to be perfect before we can speak to others about the Savior, but this is simply another of his many tactics designed to keep Christians from witnessing. It is when we recognize that we are not adequate in and of ourselves, but rely on God's strength and believe that His power is able to flow through us.

God's Role/Our Role in Evangelism

A third means to overcoming this barrier is to distinguish between God's role and our role in evangelism. There are two basic principles in evangelism: first, God does it. Second, He uses people. John 3:16, the most widely known verse in the Bible, speaks of God's love in sending His Son, but the question remains, "How did God intend to communicate His love to the masses of people?"

It is interesting to speculate on how God could have chosen to communicate with us. He could have written the plan of salvation in the heavens, using the stars. He could have carved the truths of the Gospel onto tablets like the Ten Commandments and dropped one in every city and village of the world! Since He is God, He had unlimited options at His disposal.

What Plan Did He Choose?

Someone has imagined the scene when Jesus ascended back to heaven after His death and resurrection and encountered the angel Gabriel.[28] Gabriel was extremely interested in what Jesus had been doing on earth. Jesus responded by explaining that while on earth, He had died on a cross to save people from their sins, and He had been raised up by God's power. He had now returned to heaven to take His place at God's right hand to intercede for those whom He had come to save. Jesus concluded by saying that it is His desire that all people everywhere hear the message of what He has done for them.

Gabriel asked, "And what is your plan for accomplishing this?" Jesus responded, "I have left the message in the hands of a dozen or so disciples. I am trusting them to spread it everywhere." Gabriel exclaimed, "Twelve disciples? What if they fail?" Jesus replied, "I have no other plan." Regardless of the imaginary aspect of the story, the main point is

---

28. Roy Fish, *Study Guide to the Master Plan of Evangelism* (Fleming H. Revell: Old Tappan, New Jersey, 1972), 44.

true. Jesus did leave the task of evangelizing in the hands of a small number of people. But they so thoroughly trained others to bear effective witness that soon large numbers of trained disciples were sharing the truth about Jesus all over Jerusalem, Samaria, Galilee and ultimately in the uttermost parts of the earth. We—who name the name of Christ—are here today because of the faithfulness of those early disciples.

We must keep in clear perspective what our role is and what God's role is. Paul portrays this beautifully in 1 Corinthians 3:6 when he says, "I planted the seed, Apollos watered it, but God made it grow." We are called to plant and water, but only God can give the growth. Although it is our responsibility to share the Gospel with others, it is the Holy Spirit's role to convict and convince the person of the truth of God's Word. This takes away the guilt of so-called evangelism "failures." As Bill Bright, the founder of Campus Crusade for Christ, said, "Successful witnessing is simply taking the initiative to share Christ in the power of the Holy Spirit and leaving the results to God."[29]

---

29. Bill Bright, "The Evangelist's Personal Witness," *The Calling of an Evangelist*, (World Wide Publications: Minneapolis, Minnesota, 1987), 30.

Finally, if you know your life is out of line, then do what it takes to get it back in line. Are you suffering from spiritual burnout because you have left your first love? Restore that relationship with the Lord today. Are you out of fellowship with others? Attempting to "go it alone" in the Christian life will always lead to failure and discouragement. God designed His church to provide support and encouragement for believers.

Relational Evangelism Takes Faith

Begin reaching out where you are! Beginning a lifestyle of witnessing takes faith; it will stretch you and cause you to grow! It will make demands on you that will cause you to grow in your prayer life. Have you ever heard of anyone discussing the difference between the Sea of Galilee and the Dead Sea? Both have an intake of pure water. The difference is that the Dead Sea has no outlet. The water stalls within the lake and grows stagnant and stale.

Some Christians' lives are like that. Their problem is not intake but output. They are taking in good spiritual food, but with no outlet, their lives are growing stale and stagnant. A consistent lifestyle of reaching out to others with the love of Christ is one of the keys to spiritual health.

A consistent life is important. But remember that it is not your life, but the Gospel that is "the power of God" to bring people to salvation (1 Corinthians 1:18). We must point people beyond our own lives to the cross of Christ. Like Paul, our testimony must be, "We do not preach ourselves, but Jesus Christ as Lord" (2 Corinthians 4:5).

Breaking the Barrier of Busyness

Have you ever wished for a twenty-five hour day? Have you ever felt it is impossible to cram everything you need and want to do into your current schedule? Do you ever find yourself saying, "I'd witness more, but I just can't seem to find the time!"? If you are like most people, the issue of time is a significant one. Most people in our society lead busy lives. Most of us have unanswered emails, unfinished "to-do lists," unfulfilled promises, and the list goes on and on. In addition to our own plans, others place demands on our time. Someone has remarked that the fifth spiritual law is "God loves you, and everyone else has a wonderful plan for your life." Have you ever felt like that?

Making Time/Not Finding Time

If we are to have success in breaking the barrier of busyness, the first step is to recognize an important truth. The statement we often make, "I didn't have time for this or that," is seldom true. A more accurate statement would be, "This whatever was not high enough on my priority list that I would set aside something else to do it." We never "find" time to do anything—rather, we "make" time. As one person has observed, "Time flies on its own. It's up to us to be the navigator." We choose how to spend our time based on what's important to us.

God's Perspective on Time and Eternity

A second step to breaking the barrier of busyness is to allow God to develop in us a proper perspective on time and eternity. Time is one of God's most precious gifts to us. Life at its longest is brief. James 4:14 says our life is like "a mist that appears for a little while and then vanishes." Job 7:6 refers to the passing of time as "swifter than a weaver's shuttle." Is it any wonder that in light of the brevity of life Moses prayed in Psalm 90:12, "Teach us to number our days aright, that we may gain a heart of wisdom"?

Our time is not our own; we are merely stewards of the time that God has given us. We are reminded in 1 Corinthians 6:19–20 that as followers of Christ, we are not our own—we have been bought with a price. In light of that, we need to live our lives and spend our time in the way God desires. God's plan for our lives is not merely existence! If God's only purpose in saving us was to get us to heaven, He could just "zap" us there at the moment of conversion. But He has a greater plan and purpose for our lives—that we give ourselves in loving service to others.

The philosopher, William James, once said, "The great use of life is to spend it for something that outlasts it."[30] Our Lord said, "Do not work for food that spoils, but for food that endures to eternal life" (John 6:27). Have you ever stopped to ask yourself what in this world is eternal? Pleasure? No! People are eternal. Every person on this planet will exist forever, either living in heaven with God or dying in hell separated from Him. Hebrews 9:27 tells us that everyone "is destined to die once, and after that to face judgment." In John 5:28–29, Jesus says, "Do not be amazed at this, for

30. William James, *The Encyclopedia of Religious Quotations* (Fleming H. Revell Company: Old Tappan, New Jersey, 1965), 270.

a time is coming when all who are in their graves will hear His voice and come out—those who have done good will rise to live, and those who have done evil will rise to be condemned." People are eternal! How we need for God to burden each of our hearts with this reality—there is nothing on earth more important than people.

Many people are giving their time and their lives to accumulate things that God has already promised to destroy. 2 Peter 3:10 tells us that when the Lord returns like a thief in the night, "the earth and everything in it will be laid bare." Jesus challenged His followers by saying, "Do not store up for yourselves treasures on earth, where moth and rust destroy, and where thieves break in and steal. But store up for yourselves treasures in heaven, where moth and rust do not destroy, and where thieves do not break in and steal. For where your treasure is, there your heart will be also" (Matthew 6:19–21). Where is your treasure? Scripture challenges us to make our treasure that which is eternal—not temporal. People are eternal!

If you are like most believers, you face a tremendous struggle when it comes to spending time with other people. You have friends at church with whom you desire to fellowship, and there never seems to be enough time for that. And yet you know you need to try to reach out to lost people as well! How can you possibly manage all this? We must strive for balance. We need fellowship. We vitally need the encouragement and support we receive from other believers. But we also need to be involved in ministry and in reaching out to others. We need to make "the most of every opportunity, because the days are evil" (Ephesians 5:16).

Managing Time

Once we have begun to gain a sense of God's priorities for our lives, what other practical steps can we take to break through the barrier of busyness? The following are some general principles of time management which have proven helpful:

The first step to managing time is to identify time wasters. Analyze how you are currently spending your time. Keep a log for a week. You will be surprised at how many "time robbers" you can identify. Perhaps the biggest "time robber" in our society is our smartphone. RescueTime, an app that monitors phone use, reports that people spend an average of three hours and 15 minutes on their phones every day.[31] This equates to over 22 hours a week.

The Church of England on Norfolk Island shared this on their Facebook page:

My SmartPhone is my shepherd;
I still want more.
I stare at it in green pastures,
I text instead of looking at the still waters.
It drains my soul;
It leads me in the paths of unrighteousness
For the apps sake.
Yea, though I walk through the valley of No Likes,
I will not fear;
For my SmartPhone is with me;
Snapchat and Instagram, they comfort me.
My SmartPhone prepares a fake world for me in
the presence of reality;
It anoints my head with secular humanism;
My discontent runs over.
Surely laziness and comparison shall follow me
all the days of my life;

---

31. https://blog.rescuetime.com/screen-time-stats-2018/

And I will dwell in the Cyberworld
Looking down at my Smartphone
Forever.[32]

This is certainly not to say that smartphones in and of themselves are evil. But can a Christian possibly justify spending over twenty hours a week scrolling on the internet? Do we want to waste our brief lives on earth searching cute cat memes? Wouldn't we rather cut down on our entertainment and have more time for people— for people who are eternal?

Besides entertainment, other common "time robbers" are failing to plan and procrastinating. What are your "time robbers"? Develop plans for eliminating or reducing them. It is a simple truth—if we want to add something to our schedule, we must first subtract something. And what better thing to subtract than time that is being "wasted"? More time is wasted in minutes than hours. We think, "A minute here, a few minutes there—that isn't all too significant." Lord Chesterfield once observed, "Take care

---

32. https://www.facebook.com/948976061793326/posts/my-smartphone-is-my-shepherdi-still-want-morei-stare-at-it-in-green-pasturesi-te/2279635128727406/

of the minutes, and the hours will take care of themselves."[33]

Having identified "time robbers," a second important principle of time management is to operate on a schedule. Having a schedule gives you the freedom to say, "No!" Some people say, "I care too much about others to schedule my time. I want to be available to people whenever they need me." The only problem with that statement is it seldom works out that way. Those who have a schedule somehow seem to make time for people when others can never find the time. A schedule is not sacred; it can always be changed if important needs arise. But without a schedule, we are left open to the whims of circumstances. A written schedule can help us to plan our time each day, week and month, making sure we schedule time in light of our priorities—especially time with people. People are eternal.

A third suggestion is to be creative in your use of time. Learn to do two things at once. What activities can you do with people as you are building relationships with them? Use your leisure

---

33. Lord Chesterfield, (Lord Chesterfield, letter to his son October 9, 1746), *A New Dictionary of Quotations* (published by Alfred A. Knopf Inc. 1941), 790.

time creatively. Take your unsaved friends to a ball game or a concert. Suggest a family picnic together, or take the kids to a playground. Have a neighborhood barbecue in your backyard. The possibilities are endless if we will only have eyes to see.

Where Do I Begin?

As you seek to overcome these common barriers to witnessing, you may wonder, "Where do I begin in reaching out to lost people?" You will want to assess where you are now. Do you currently know any non-Christians? Begin by praying for your neighborhood, workplace, or school, wherever you spend most of your time each day. God knows the responsive hearts in your sphere of influence. How do you locate them?

Make an Initial Acquaintance

Build relationships with people near you. As you do so, you will become aware of those who are ready to respond to the Gospel. It all begins by making an initial acquaintance. The actual moment when you can share the Gospel may not come until months later—after a friendship has been established. We are surrounded by people who are spiritually hungry. True, you cannot minister to everyone, but how about extending your friendship to four or five individuals in your daily life. You may discover that two or three of these will be responsive.

Establish a Growing Relationship

Once you have made the initial acquaintance, you may question, "How do I build a relationship with this person?"

• Ask God to help you get to know others. Get to know names and be sure to pronounce them correctly.

• Second, smile! Be the kind of person those around you would want to know. If you desire to build redemptive friendships, be friendly.

• Third, be a good listener. Discover and discuss the interests of others rather than your own. Have one or more topics in mind that you can use to begin the conversation.

• Fourth, take the initiative to be of help when it is appropriate. If your friend is painting the house, grab a brush! Offer to mow your friend's lawn and look after the house and pets while the family is on vacation.

Extend an Invitation to Your Home

Your goal is to advance your daily contacts with those near you toward a more significant friendship. Meals are a great way to do it. Have you ever noticed how much of Jesus' ministry took place over meals? Remember what the Pharisees asked Jesus' disciples, "Why do you eat and drink with tax collectors and sinners?" (Luke 5:30). When was the last time you had non-Christians in your home for a meal? If we are to follow the pattern of Jesus in reaching out to others, mealtimes are a good place to begin. Most of us schedule time to eat meals during the day. Why not use the time you have already set aside in your schedule to reach out to people who need to hear the Gospel of Christ?

What to Say/What Not to Say

When your non-Christian friends are over for dinner, don't feel compelled to "say" something spiritual. Many seem to think that if they have not shared their "witness" before the evening is over, they have failed. Not so. It usually takes time to cultivate a friendship to the point where their hearts are ready to hear and receive the message.

However, you should say grace at the meal. It is your home, and it is natural for you to do this. Do not preach or share a quick "witness" during prayer. Rather, be brief and thank the Lord for your friends by name.

Cultivate Common Interests

Your goal is to build a reservoir of common shared experiences with people near you whom you desire to introduce to Christ. Sometimes it is good to think through a list of possible common-ground "contact points." Begin by making a list of possible activities or common interests, for example: gardening, skiing, tennis, boating, hunting, fishing, sewing, crafts, movies, concerts, and the list goes on and on. Then put a check by those which would be options for you as you seek to do things together. You will want to include only those items on your list which both you and your friends would enjoy. It is important to discover these "contact points" and use them as friendship building-blocks.

Be Available for the Hurting

Is there anyone hurting in your neighborhood? This is another way you can make contact with non-Christians who need a true friend and to whom you can introduce the Lord Jesus. Life is tough. Sickness, death of a loved one, marital problems, financial difficulties, and other pressures provide opportunities for the Christian to express Christ's love through caring, sharing and serving. Remember, people do not care how much (or what) you know until they know how much you care. The hurts of others are your opportunities to bring the Good News to them. These opportunities are often arranged by God Himself. In lifestyle or friendship evangelism, availability is often the greatest ability. Be a listening, sensitive, giving, caring, Christian friend. When you make yourself available to God, He will surely use you!

Become a Giver

You can make an impact on those around you by being creative in your use of Christian resources. Give your friends something to listen to or read. Be casual about it. When entertaining, put some good Christian literature on your coffee table. Stick with Christian books and magazines that are need-centered and have good graphics. There are also some challenging videos which are effective in evangelism. Be sure, however, that you watch the video first! It should be positive in tone and attitude, need-centered, and biblically sound. Purchase a supply of quality items and keep them readily available to give to your non-Christian friends when the time is right.

Find an Appropriate Harvest Vehicle

After you have spent time with your non-Christian friends, discovered their interests, developed a friendship, and helped to meet their needs, there comes a time to take that next step! There comes a time when it is appropriate to pray about involving them in some type of ministry vehicle. A sensitivity toward their preferences and personal views is important. If there must be an offense, let it be the offense of the Gospel, not the manner in which the Gospel is presented.

There are numerous "harvest vehicles." For example: evangelistic dinners, home Bible studies, business breakfasts, Christian movies, conferences or retreats, fishing/hunting trips, church sports programs, and the list goes on and on. Once you have found the "right" harvest vehicle for your non-Christian friends, invite them to go with you.

Remember, *effective evangelism is built on relationships*. One person who has found new life, meaning and forgiveness through an encounter with Jesus Christ is motivated by love to bring another to experience that same relationship with the Savior. Most Christians can point to a caring person who prayed for them or in some way or another helped bring them to the Lord. You can be that kind of caring person too.

Conclusion

In the previous six chapters, we have looked at "Overcoming Walls to Witnessing." We have examined how we can break through the barriers of fear, giftedness, ignorance, apathy, introspection, and busyness. Are you willing, with God's help, to break through the barriers in your life that are keeping you from sharing Christ with others? Will you no longer say, "Someday I'll do it," but make "someday" today?

An essay titled *Do It Now* sums up how too many of us approach life—always putting things off until tomorrow. The essay says:

> *He was going to be all that a mortal should be—*
> *Tomorrow.*
> *No one should be kinder or braver than he—*
> *Tomorrow.*

A friend who was troubled and weary he knew.
Who'd be glad of a lift, and who needed it too;
On him he would call and see what he could do—
Tomorrow.
Each morning he stacked up the letters he'd write—
Tomorrow.
And thought of the folks he would fill with delight—
Tomorrow.
It was too bad, indeed, he was busy today
And hadn't a minute to stop on his way;
More time he would have to give others, he'd say—
Tomorrow.
The greatest of workers this man would have been—
Tomorrow.
The world would have known him had he ever seen—
Tomorrow.
But the fact is, he died, and he faded from view,
And all that he left when living was through
Was a mountain of things he intended to do—
Tomorrow.[34]

Do you ever wish for a twenty-five hour day? That wouldn't solve the problem. Our hectic lifestyle would soon expand to consume that extra hour.

---

34. Gene Warr, *A Teacher's Guide to the Godly Man* (28:19, Inc.: Oklahoma City, Oklahoma, 1975), 49.

If we are going to accomplish anything in life, it will have to be done not tomorrow, when we mistakenly think our lives somehow will settle down, but today, in the midst of our busyness. We all make time to do what we really want to do, what is really important to us. Will you allow God to burden your heart for lost people? Will you make some time today, to begin reaching out to someone with the love of Christ? People are eternal!

Resource List

1. J Mack Stiles, *Evangelism* (Crossway).
2. Roger Carswell, *Evangelistic Living* (10Publishing).
3. John S Leonard, *Get Real* (New Growth Press).
4. John Lennox, *Have No Fear* (10Publishing).
5. Rico Tice, *Honest Evangelism* (The Good Book Company).
6. Paul Williams, *Intentional* (10Publishing).
7. Jerram Barrs, *Learning Evangelism from Jesus* (Crossway).
8. Becky Manly Pippert, *Out of the Saltshaker* (IVP).
9. Becky Manly Pippert, *Stay Salt* (The Good Book Company).
10. Robert E. Coleman, *The Master Plan of Evangelism* (Baker).

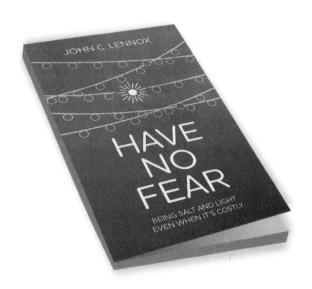

10Publishing is the publishing house of 10ofThose. It is committed to producing quality Christian resources that are biblical and accessible.

www.10ofthose.com is our online retail arm selling thousands of quality books at discounted prices.

For information contact: info@10ofthose.com
or check out our website: www.10ofthose.com